READ THEN THINK

IT'S NOT ONLY A BOOK BUT IT'S MY FEELING

ASHISH KUMAR

No.8, 3rd Cross Street, CIT Colony,
Mylapore, Chennai, Tamil Nadu-600004

Copyright © Ashish Kumar
All Rights Reserved.

ISBN 978-1-64919-165-6

This book has been published with all efforts taken to make the material error-free after the consent of the author. However, the author and the publisher do not assume and hereby disclaim any liability to any party for any loss, damage, or disruption caused by errors or omissions, whether such errors or omissions result from negligence, accident, or any other cause.

While every effort has been made to avoid any mistake or omission, this publication is being sold on the condition and understanding that neither the author nor the publishers or printers would be liable in any manner to any person by reason of any mistake or omission in this publication or for any action taken or omitted to be taken or advice rendered or accepted on the basis of this work. For any defect in printing or binding the publishers will be liable only to replace the defective copy by another copy of this work then available.

To my friend-cum-boss Heena Chugh

99% motivation & 99% patience

No, it does not add upto 198% but she multitasks.

Contents

Preface	*vii*
Acknowledgements	*ix*
1. Note Worthy	1
2. Life Is A Mixture	2
3. Some People	3
4. Fine	4
5. Entertainment	5
6. Circumstances	6
7. I Don't Have Enough Time	7
8. Dear Death	8
9. Dear Heart	10
10. Parents	11
11. Relationship	12
12. Fault	13
13. No Need	14
14. Separate	15
15. Wings	16
16. Excuses	17
17. Rose	18
18. Is It Right To Ignore Our Birth Givers ?	19
19. Meet Me When	20
20. If You Want	22
21. Sharper	23
22. Satisfaction	24

Contents

23. Mirror	25
24. Assumption	26
25. Death & Liberation	27
26. Reflection	28
27. Worthless	29
28. Make Up Or Decoration	30
29. One More Time	31
30. I Know	32
31. Something Something	33
32. A Point In Life	34
33. Skipping A Preface	35
34. Sine Wave	36
35. Power Of A Thought	37
36. Death	38
37. Dear Someone	39
38. Dear Life	40

Preface

Here I would want to say something about the tone of this book. There is noticeably a common voice or approach. This is not a collection of vatic lyrics or dissociated rambles. The quotes are often set at a middle distance, in a voice aware that it is speaking, pondering, puzzling, but alerting as well to the impulses that are unspoken.

Quote is the most difficult form of human utterance. And when a man plays well or writes well, his audience must have intelligence, training, and patience in order to appreciate him.

These are precisely the characteristics/summary of the quotes in this book. Accuracy is not literalism or pedantry; it is the ability to see and describe things as, at first glance or second thought, they truly are. Spontaneity is not improvisation or loafing; it is a fresh apprehension of the uneven textures of life. Mystery is not profundity or spirituality; it is the ability of a quote to clear space for what couldn't before have been anticipated, even by the quote itself—the passing thought or startling image that makes a reader stop and wonder. This is what good quotes do.

In the book, I have discussed both my experiences/feelings and how they changed me. You'll find quotes and mementos that I hope will touch your heart.

Acknowledgements

Writing a book is harder than I thought and more rewarding than I could have ever imagined. None of this would have been possible without our society, who gave me multiple (multi-coloured) experiences of life.

I'm eternally grateful to **Mr. Sachin Gururani** my friend-cum-brother who has designed the beautiful cover of the book and my parents as well, who encouraged me during the entire journey of my writing.

Special thanks to **Dr. Sakshi Pal** and friends who suggested me to write a book and helped me in finalizing it within a limited time frame.

Writing a book about the reality of life is a surreal process. I'm forever indebted to my incredible readers as this has become possible because of their efforts and encouragement.

Finally, thanks to all those who have been a part of this beautiful journey.

1. NOTE WORTHY

Respect your Parents, and,
There's no need to worship any God,
Your luck will grow Everyday.

2. LIFE IS A MIXTURE

Life is a Mixture
of Happiness and Sadness.
Enjoy the Happiness and be valorous
Enough to face sadness.
Without hitting the lowest
You will never understand.
Happiness after Sadness
Is always enjoyable.

3. SOME PEOPLE

Some People act as
If they know everything
On this planet!
And "I don't know" never exists
In their dictionary.

4. FINE

Everything will be fine.
If you change your view.

5. ENTERTAINMENT

Many people believe that
Playing with feelings
Is a good source of
Entertainment.

6. CIRCUMSTANCES

Don't treat yourself
As a slave of circumstances.
You are the creator
Of your own destiny.
Just, go ahead
And rock the world....!!!!

7. I DON'T HAVE ENOUGH TIME

I don't have enough
Time to waste and spend
With people who don't
Even want to talk to me.
But being friendly
With everyone is the main thing.
Forwarding a hand
Of friendship towards people
Is my habit which sometimes,
Turns enemies into good friends.

8. DEAR DEATH

Dear Death,
I am so glad that I can talk to you now.
How lucky I am!
I have one question.
What happens to me after I die?
Do you really take my soul away
or take me from the people who need me?
When will you come?
Please don't knock the door.
Come silently & give me a packet of little hearts
OR
Just give me a Milky Bar chocolate.
And whisper
"You have to leave right now"
I promise you,
I will not make any excuse
Nor will I take time.
My dear death,
Please don't give me pain
Because there is already too much pain in my life..
I know,
You are my final destination

*This life is a journey
where
Happiness & Sadness are my partners.
I know everything
Yet I am afraid of you.
There are too many sad moments in this path of life
But
It is also true that
there is immense happiness in my mother's food.
I know my lovely death,
You are the Unspoken truth that everybody knows, still don't accept.*

9. DEAR HEART

Dear Heart,
How are you???
I know you are not good.
I'm writing this letter to catch your attention.
Control your feelings because no one will be
With you till the end.
You are not doing your job perfectly.
You are too weak dear.
Try to work like an organ.
Pump blood not emotions.
Have you understood?
Beat in synchrony.
Just stop skipping beats.
The Mind is there to lead,
Control yourself
Or else
You would break and bleed!

10. PARENTS

Parents are the rays of light,
They enlighten the dark places.
If you cut the source of light,
You can't overcome darkness.

11. RELATIONSHIP

It takes a few moments
to ruin a relationship
But,
A whole life is invested
To build it.

12. FAULT

The fault was not
In the castes.
The fault was
In their mentality.

13. NO NEED

Be the way you are.
There's no need to change yourself
In order to impress people
Because people will change once
They have gained what they wanted from you.

14. SEPARATE

Miles don't separate.
But
Misunderstandings do.

15. WINGS

You don't need anyone else's wings.
You own your own pair of wings.
Let them free.
And,
Fly away in the open sky.

16. EXCUSES

Don't give excuses,
To run away
From the difficulties.
Be brave
Find a way
And face them
With a bang.

17. ROSE

Instead of gifting a rose
To someone.
Spread your fragrance
Like a rose
Let the whole world
Know you.

18. IS IT RIGHT TO IGNORE OUR BIRTH GIVERS ?

We never give a single rose to our parents
But
We give a bunch of roses to our lover

Is it right to ignore our birth givers?

19. MEET ME WHEN

Meet me when
You are ready to give me a milky bar
Meet me when
My dreams look broken
Meet me when
I start recollecting my happy moments
Meet me when
I'm unable to recognize myself
Meet me when
You can understand my pain
Meet me when
I don't have any tears in my eyes
Meet me when
I can't utter a single word
Meet me when
I can't listen a single voice
Meet me when
My heart has stopped working
Meet me when
I'm free from all responsibilities
Meet me when
Everyone is ready to give me a shoulder

ASHISH KUMAR

Meet me when
I stop writing
Simply
Meet me when
My body & soul will separate

20. IF YOU WANT

If you want to reach
The peak of success,
Then enhance your self-confidence
And give-up your despair immediately.
Because,
The Initiative is Life
And Infirmity is death.

21. SHARPER

Someone asked me if there's
Anything sharper than a sword.

*I replied **"Yes, it's the tongue."***

22. SATISFACTION

Those who are satisfied
With their work
And have no desire
To earn progress,
Will never grow in their future.

23. MIRROR

Whenever I look at the mirror,
I realize that it is impossible
To fulfil our persistent desires.

24. ASSUMPTION

Life is a reality, not an assumption.
So, never try to assume anything.

25. DEATH & LIBERATION

There is a slight difference
Between Death & liberation
If the world leaves you
Then you are dead
But If you leave the world
Then you are liberated.

26. REFLECTION

Behaviour is the reflection
of your personality,
The kind of person you are.
But, oversmartness is the reflection
of what you are trying to be.

27. WORTHLESS

It is worthless
To express your feelings
Where your feelings
Are not valued.

28. MAKE UP OR DECORATION

The make up
Of the body falls apart at night.
But if you decorate
Your soul once,
Even after death,
it cannot disintegrate.

29. ONE MORE TIME

Do not give up,
Even if you fail.
Try one more time,
Just one more.
I'm sure,
You will definitely get success.

30. I KNOW

I know you are there
Somewhere near.
I know you are around me
Whenever I hear.
I know you care
But you never share.
I know you miss me
But you don't piss me
I know you wanna hold me tight
Whenever we fight.
I know you'll always be with me
Whenever I need you with me.

31. SOMETHING SOMETHING

When Eyes Meet
Hearts Beat
It Is Something Something
When Smiles Meet
Hearts Beat
It Is Something Something
&
We Are Desperately Waiting
To Hear That
'Something Something'
One More Time
Please Come Back
Together With A Bang
Lots of love and warm wishes
From the bottom of my heart.

32. A POINT IN LIFE

There comes a point
In life where
One wants to cry
But tears fail to flow.

33. SKIPPING A PREFACE

Many people skipped me
Like a preface
And then, they tried to read
Whole book but failed to
Find my fragrance.

34. SINE WAVE

Life is like a sine wave
It is full of ups and downs
So, don't be a constant, be a variable.

35. POWER OF A THOUGHT

There is nothing
In the world that can harm you
Except your own thinking.
Because it is said that
Only a thought can lead you
To your development or destruction.

36. DEATH

Fear of death
Is more dangerous
Than death itself.

37. DEAR SOMEONE

Dear Someone,

You hurt me, then you say 'sorry.'
But you hurt me again.
You said, "You don't love me."
But, then, you show me some love.
After this, you ignore me like a plague.
You treat me just like a toy,
The one you need when you are bored and once,
You find something entertaining, you throw it away.
Just like the thing that you picked up
When it was needed but later, it became useless.
My heart aches every time
Because you never understand my problem.
Yet, I want you to be with me and your arms to die in.
JUST WANT YOU TO BE ONLY MINE.
Dear, I still love you immensely.
But, at the same time,
I'm sure you will never understand me or my love
Because you are a child & a child always play with a toy
And for you, I am just a toy.

38. DEAR LIFE

Dear Life,
Hi!
How are you?
I hope, you are doing great.
It's been three years and you haven't contacted me once.
I know, leaving me, was totally your decision,
A decision taken carefully, but like a fool (that I am),
I waited for you just in a hope that one day,
You would think about me
And all those lovely memories, we created.
Guess, I was wrong.
Anyway, I am sorry,
I didn't want to disturb you like this,
But, I got to know about your wedding
And was dying of curiosity.
I just want to know about you and him?
How is he?
Is he a good looking guy or a cute one?
Or the muscular one?
Is he taller than me
Or the one who suits your height?
Is he an IIT engineer or a UPSC aspirant or Doctor?

Apologies in advance,
But, I want to know everything.
How have you exactly felt,
When you deleted my name like
A corrupted file from your life
And accepted him as your life partner?
Were the both names written
The same way on the wedding card
As we had thought of ours?
Were you happy when he held your hands around the fire,
Taking vows to stay together?
Did your tears tell our incomplete story
Or were you happy for a new beginning?
Does he kiss you on the forehead
To make your day
Or do you still miss our morning hug?
Does he prepare morning tea for you
Or do you still miss my breakfast in bed?
Is he a good boy,
Who puts the things in proper place
Or just messes with things like me?
Does he bite your fingers
When you feed him with your hand
Or make faces when you add extra salt in?
Does he like when you wear a western outfit
Or force you to wear only Indian attires?
Does he go out with you

And carry your shopping bags
Or only pay for it?
I want to know,
Is he able to handle your mood swings
Or gets irritated easily?
Does he like to move his hands
Between your silky hair or find it boring?
Does he pamper you during menstruation period
Or feel bothered?
Does he make ugly faces
In your selfies
Or give perfect pose?
Does he put your mobile on charging
When you play late night games
Or just leave it with you?
Does his love and care make you happy
Or you miss my care?
Do you enjoy his car rides
Or miss my bike rides?
Have you really fallen in love with him
Or still have feelings for me?
Who am I for you?
A sweet memory
Or the worst nightmare?
Honestly, it doesn't matter,
Whatever I am to you.
You are still the same for me.

The one, whom I loved with all my heart
And will always love till the last breath.
May be we were never meant
To be together yet the days
We have spent together hold the greatest memories.
Heartiest congratulations on your new life.
Don't worry, I am happy in my life.
My family is there to shower their love and never-ending blessings.
Enclosing with love and warm wishes.

Life is like a Book
The more you Live it
The more it's pages will Grow

www.ingramcontent.com/pod-product-compliance
Lightning Source LLC
LaVergne TN
LVHW021739060526
838200LV00052B/3354